THE PAINKILLER

WITH NO SIDE EFFECTS

The Painkiller With No Side Effects
Prafful Garg
Print Edition

First Published & Printed in India in 2021
Inkfeathers Publishing, New Delhi 110095
Copyright © Prafful Garg, 2021
Book & Cover Design © Prafful Garg, 2021

THE PAINKILLER

WITH NO SIDE EFFECTS

PRAFFUL GARG

Inkfeathers Publishing

For GEN-Z,

to be stronger than they were till date and

my pillars of strength, my dad

Mr. VIPIN GARG

&

KHATU SHYAM BABA

Contents

Introduction

The Generation-Z is born in an era which is crucial for not only the individuals but also the country, the continent, and the world we live in. This book is written to grow the young minds in a stronger self, who is unbeatable by the outer world until it has lost the battle to the world inside.

Gen-Z works on multiple skill-sets through which they get drained daily, but still feel that things are not moving. This book will be a deep self-realization for them, showing that they are growing daily whether it's in their school, college or workplace. But what is growing above all is the mindset; the brain which looks beyond what can be seen.

The division is into three sections.

YOU, it's all about one's own self, the depth of which cannot be measured.

Then we move to YOURS which talk about all our worldly relations, few of which are made by God, and others by humans themselves. It also talks about the depth of each relation as a whole.

The third chapter is about OURS, the world which is not around us but still has a huge impact on us, either directly or through others. It also covers various unspoken topics which are important to us, but which we majorly tend to ignore.

The one thing to watch out for in this book are the explanations of the multiple thoughts which work on my concept of 'look beyond'. The explanations are full of meanings which are understood but not totally comprehended by the Gen-Z today.

How to be good enough at everything we do? Maybe you don't have an answer to this question right now, but you will have one by the end of this book, probably!

You

__Building thoughts or Burning fuel of the world inside us i.e. 'YOU' will drive you to eternal success.__

Generation Z uses the word **'OP'**, short for **'Overpowered'** frequently. Well, the power which you generate being around people, or from them, is not sustainable because it's fuelled by the energy of the world around you, not the energy of the world inside you.

> ***Sometimes things do not make sense. Because things need to make sense in imagination not in reality.***

We want things to make sense in our imagination, but the question is whether you get a sense of accomplishment in your imagination or physical reality?

Bravo! You can accomplish something only in reality!

You can either cry oceans to sleep or wake up to a mountain of thoughts.

When you cry in front of someone, often you feel embarrassed, and would probably avoid eye contact with that person for a while. And when you cry alone, your emotions flow, your eyes burn. But if you don't cry in the night and sleep tight, you have plethora of thoughts running down your body. They help you get out of bed early in the morning to make the bright part of the day productive.

I'm done with fake people and that includes the fake version of myself.

Actions speak louder than words, but when it comes to recognizing fake people's actions and words, both are fake, but the vibe is real. You don't need to give a second chance to understand a person's vibe. Therefore, whenever you meet someone new, trust their vibe and not their actions or words. I hope after reading this you will not try to be fake, because fake is not impressive but depressive.

Are you ok?
I'm ok ok.

Sometimes you yourself don't know whether you are okay or not. You are in that zone where you don't know how you are feeling. We sometimes taste food and don't know whether it tastes good or bad and we end up saying it's ok ok. The thing or person who turns your ok ok mood to ok is something you should have or someone you should meet more often. It would be the best if you set yourself right on your own.

When you want to beg, beg but to yourself not to someone else.

When you beg someone for something, you put something at stake, which can't be bought back by even money, i.e. Respect. You should beg yourself for willpower and everything else will follow. Having said that, trust me on this, never stop begging your parents for money even when you make more than them. Because it reminds them of your childhood when they were everything for you and they didn't have to share you with anyone. As it is said that no matter how much you grow for your parents you will stay a child, so act like one.

"You mean the world to me."
Say this to yourself three times a day and
keep the doctors and psychologists away.

Healthy eating is required to keep the doctors away and healthy living is required to keep the psychologists away. An invisible wound is healed by the ray of hope which is not coming from the world outside but from the world within you.

The world can call me mean but yes, I mean the world to myself.

Mind your own business,
Grow your own mind.

When you have 10,000$ and someone stole 1000$, will you give up on the left-over 9000$ for those 1000$? No right, then why do you give away all the positivity within you because of one negativity (in the form of person or thing) around you.

You grow mature when you don't mind minding your own business, ONLY!

You can accept your own apology.

You say sorry for something and plan not to repeat it. Go take the risk! If you get the reward, Great! If not, say sorry to yourself and learn from that mistake. We say sorry to the world thousand times in a day but to ourselves maybe not even once. Why? We should.

Let's go a bit deeper, if you learn to forgive yourself maybe you will learn to forgive others even faster because you will understand the importance of sorry and forgiveness together forever.

Who are you? I answered to the person but could not to the mirror.

We talk about the concept of being real, but it's not 100% practically possible. We are human race which tries to prove the best versions of themselves in front of the world. That's why, answering before people, known or unknown, is easy. But when we talk to ourselves, we talk 100% reality because lying to yourself is better termed as fooling yourself.

I know we sometimes try to fool ourselves off the reality but that's a temporary solution. You may do that to find peace, but when that silence will break, it will break with the sound of the glass. DON'T FOOL YOURSELF!

You aren't ready yet.
'Yet' is till the last fraction of a second.
This fraction of second changes
everything. Don't give up, instead, pick
it up!

We give up on nearly ten new opportunities daily, because we think we are not ready. The harsh reality is, we will never be ready, because there is no parameter to understand when you are challenge or change ready. There is only one way to get ready and that is to Pick it up and not Give up. Give yourself to the mission!

When one is angry at you, they either care for you or they don't. Try to plot the latter and cut off from them completely and do vice-versa with the other.

The one who cares for you will get angry and after a while, they will come back and tell you the reason for the same. But the one who doesn't, will get angry and next time will make sure that they are louder.

There is a very sleek difference between being angry at someone and showing that anger & being angry at someone and disrespecting you. The latter is out for today and forever.

Personality is not all about the body, if you want to build it, grow both mind and brain not OR.

Sometimes we love spending time with our uncle or aunt who are 60+. It doesn't feel that they were born In 1950's, that is the magic of a personality which is made of evolving thoughts. Eye-contact speaks a lot about a person's confidence and their personality. Real personality check is not in front of the knowns but from the opinions of the unknown about you after the first meeting. Reading helps you build a good personality. I'm talking about reading people, their body language, eyes, and everything which you can read along with words and facial expression.

Waking up to the same thought you slept with is RARE.

Gen-Z has something which is strangely different from the other generations. They have multiple thoughts running up and down their minds every night when they go to sleep, and they don't think about them with the same intensity of concern in the morning. This is Overthinking, where thoughts just don't let you sleep. These thoughts are unnecessary and unwanted, like a person day-dreaming in the middle of the night.

On the other hand, if you think about something all night and wake up to it because it's time to work on it, that's good news. It means you overthought in the right direction.

It's not a thought, it's a purpose.

Wildfire is there one in the forest where it's difficult to reach and there's one inside me which is difficult to see.

The wildfire gets famous because of the damage it causes, the difficulty the world has to face to snuff it out, the animals which die and the species we lose. The wildfire inside you should be equally dangerous but for good. There is a fire inside many of us, but only few are able to reach to the top, because that fire generates desperation inside one and urges them to achieve something big as early as possible, but in some, it generates patience who use it at the right time for the right purpose.

You can either use that fire to burn others seeing your success or get burned in it, because only those who can use fire knows how to play with it otherwise don't forget the burn leaves lifetime marks.

I will stay strong today and forever, no conditions applied.

Many times, someone else becomes our strength or whatever we do is more for them and less for us. It's good to have someone whom you love so much and they should be there to strengthen your strength to reach your goals.

You should have your close ones there when you run the marathon and I know you will need their support in the last few miles. But never forget who made you stand there on the starting line, and who got you to cover the many first miles. It was and it should be the strength within, which I term WILLPOWER.

Only Amen won't help, you will have to say I'm in.

Ask God to keep you positive always so that you can achieve what others ask from him. People are looking for God only in their bad phase of life. Trust me, in your bad phase, look out for solutions to your problems, and during your good days, talk to God each day and ask him to keep you optimistic now and forever because that happiness will surely help you build sustainability in life.

When you pray to God and think he will give you everything is just short-lived mental satisfaction. Say Amen and hustle in your life to find real satisfaction.

Enough, you have seen!
Enough, you have failed!
Enough, you have cried!
Enough, you have felt lost!
Enough. Now is the time to get up
and get more than what is enough
for anyone or everyone else!

If you don't make excuses and you someday say 'It's Enough! Now it's my turn', you will start the journey of forever. I won't say you will easily reach your goal from there because it's tough, but I have assumed first that you don't make excuses.

"You are the apple of my eye."
Some see your goals and some see your
gold. The latter want Apple INC. and
prior wants you.
Choose wisely!

We all fall prey to praises because it feels good. Praising someone is the best way to enter that person's comfort zone by doing just one thing - sounding genuine. If you don't want to fall prey to this, just look out for one thing: why are they praising you? Half the time, you will not find an answer. and in half of the other half they will praise you more in the second time, and there they will move out of the list. The left over half-of-half is looking out for you and not your possessions.

If you used to get instant motivation when someone used to praise you, still feel that motivation but be a bit extra cautious.

Life will stay kind to you, if you will stay tough on yourself.

I know you want to live a comfortable and satisfactory life, but who says you don't find comfort and satisfaction outside your comfort zone? Comfort zone is a subjective concept because it only exists in your brain. In reality, comfort zone means 'contentment' zone. Bigger dreams mean tougher oneself because the contentment zone is far off in reality, and imagination turns into reality when you're tougher with your own self.

From today, whenever you feel down because your actions are not giving you equal results say, "Tougher me means contented me," because actions are in your hands, not the result.

I was born and brought up on the Earth, so don't try to judge me on the basis of my city, state, or country.

We sometimes try to judge people before we even see them but the internet has given a chance to everybody to grow. Though not many take this up, the people who do, are not less than anyone else. The USA is a developed nation and India is still a developing economy but major employees and executives in various corporate giants in the USA are Indians. They say it's because they are hardworking and satisfied with less pay, but I think it's because of the way they have trained their brain and have built massive adaptability.

Chance is what matters, if you won't give chance to people who came up a long journey from nowhere just with their hard work, you won't get a chance to grow your company. You cannot create an innovative company with an imitative mindset.

'I'm hiring!'
To those who thought I'm good
for nothing.

You should adapt a habit, take more motivation when people say something negative about you on your face or behind your back than from those who only say something positive. Because there is no better instant motivation than listening to people who have more belief that you will fail than the amount of confidence you have on yourself.

If you have any plans of becoming an entrepreneur then this will be a daily course of life, when your own family don't bank you then how can you expect the outsiders to be in tune. But if it all works out, trust me, the fun is to see them feeling your success even when you are not speaking about it and you can add a cherry to the cake by staying grounded.

> ***Pain is constant.***
> ***You should try not to cause pain to***
> ***someone when you are in this world,***
> ***because you already cause a lot of it***
> ***when you are born and when you die.***

Pain which is caused unintentionally can be excused as a mistake, which is not expected to be repeated. You endure pain in your professional life, but most of it helps you grow. That's just life in other words. But causing pain intentionally is inhuman, and you pay back for it in some way or the other.

The pain suffered by your mother when you were born is much harder than any other pain combined of your lifetime. Don't let it go waste, hustle hard and make her your MAIN.

Do you try to hack studies? You study in stages and pass level by level, then why do we try to hack growth?

Till 20s marks attract us the most, and after that, money attracts us the most. But did we try to clear many grades together till we got 20? No, then why do we try to get all the promotions together and find shortcuts to grow? We should set a plan and make our own school, our own grades, and our own scoreboard. , the name of this new school should be 'Financial Literacy'.

Growth is gradual or growth is gradual, Read that again. It means there is no other alternative!

You should wear a jacket as it gets cold and remove it when you feel warm. Use things not people.

We should learn to use things to help people, rather than using people to get things. There is a slight difference between taking someone's help or using them. The surprising part is we know when we are using them or taking their help. Using someone is the worst because you are dependent on them for your work and they are there in good faith. When they come to know about your bad traits, they are not hurt, they are upset, upset to be too good to someone who is too bad to be with in the first place.

I learnt how to adjust and that's why everyone adjusts with me today.

When you are growing and struggling, you cannot be the person who can be demanding. You are supposed to adjust with everything as it comes, and fulfil others' demands without complaining, because everyone has their time. You can either act in someone else's time as it is yours or wait for your own.

When you start getting successful in life, do remember how you adjusted with others in the past, and don't make people adjust with you unnecessarily, making them uncomfortable, because someone has to break the bar someday, otherwise this world of humanity will be behind bars one day.

You were powerful and then you got tamed.

Influencing is a word which got famous after the rise of social media and affiliate marketing, but it has been in business since decades. The power of influencing is either gold or coal, depending on how important it is in your life. If you get influenced by someone to the extent that whatever they say is right, and you have no questions to raise, it's like the body is yours but the brain is of someone else. Influencing is powerful for you if you take the idea from them and then use your brain whether to do it or not, that's where you build synergy with the influencer.

Never get Tamed if you want to get Fame. A lion performs on the stick of the trainer who tamed him, and the trainer never tries to even stand near the wolf, that shows the power of the mind.

Sayings

Start starting yourself,

Push pushing yourself,

Worry worrying yourself,

Love loving yourself,

Hate hating yourself,

Chase chasing yourself,

Last but not the least,

BE YOURSELF!

You hate yourself when you get the first pimple,

You hate yourself more when you get the second pimple.

But you make peace with the third one.

Hatred is temporary, self-love is permanent.

Measure your day

in minutes (1440)

not in hours (24).

Minutes move faster

and so will you.

You want to get satisfaction?

Try to live up to your own expectations

not that of others.

37

~~You live life once~~, you live life twice!

Once before committing a mistake

and one, after it!

You cannot go back and make a

Brand New Beginning.

But you can start now and make a

Never Forgotten Ending!

Risk matrix for growth:

1- Risk failure to find success.

2- Risk exhaustion to find mental health.

3- Risk experiment to find solution.

4- Risk yourself to win yourself.

Are you looking for the right person in your life? I have a

tip,

Be one!

41

It's not about winning, it's about willing.

Success comes when you stop seeking motivation

and start the execution.

Want to be fit?

Before tasting the salt in the food in the morning, taste the

salt of your sweat in the gym.

Before putting efforts to make someone else

fall in love with you, put efforts to

fall in love with yourself!

Yours

Anything which you cannot buy with money but earn with your deeds is Yours for this life and the life after.

When you create an impression it's not long lasting, but when you impress someone with your deeds i.e. who you are, you win something which is priceless, RESPECT. You should be respected by everyone who is close to you because respect is a form of love which is rare. Respect is the first thing which is compromised in a love relationship because impressions are not deeds, rather deeds are the real impressions.

Sometimes the grip is not perfect.

Relationships (whether man-made or blood relations) are not perfect, but they can be made perfect. When you are born, your grip is not even there, but your mom still tries to hit in because she wants to. If you want to, you can make the grip perfect with time. It's just that you need to feel the need of it. Half-gripping is as dangerous as half information about something.

You care so you hear when I'm quiet.

And the more astonishing fact, is you hear me when I'm sad but trying to show to the outside world that I'm happy with my smile. That's why you mean the world to me not the world.

I create the pictures which you imagine.

Maybe this thought should be dedicated to all the writers, directors, painters, creators etc. But in real-life-drama you should be the one who writes and runs a relationship because then your chances of influencing the other person are more. In short, you will not write a fairy tale but rather live in one.

Karma will play it's role, when are you playing yours?

When you meet with an accident, you first care about your wounds, and then see whose mistake it is and what will karma do. Why don't you repair your invisible wounds rather than cribbing about the heartbreak? If you take action for your growth, trust me, one day you will not have time to see the actions taken by Karma.

"You are my life", a son said.

If the above statement was said like, "You are my life", a girl said blushing to her boyfriend. Probably it might have not needed an interpretation. Then why did you look for an interpretation when a son said to his mom/dad? Your life should be for the people who gave you ONE before the people who became a part of it.

Friendship is a choice, Brotherhood is a responsibility.

With the advent of social media, the meaning of the word 'friendship' has degraded over time. You are super comfortable talking or meeting someone for the first time because you have met them over chat or video call multiple times before. But there are a few friends who become like brothers (best friend) and leaving them is not a choice and always sticking around, even when they do something wrong and helping them to get back on track is a responsibility.

When you love someone more and it ends, you hate yourself more.

When you love someone more than yourself, you end up ruining that relationship, because then, the major decisions and thoughts become impractical and insecurity grows. And when that relation turns toxic and ends, you get a self-realization of the reason being your over-involvement and losing your individuality in that relation. This makes you hate yourself more than ever, because you lost your love because of your love.

Argument or Relationship, you can win one.

We all know that we must value relationships more than arguments, but we end up losing the relationship and winning the argument. You know why? Because our ego takes control of our mind without our permission and makes us do things which we might regret later.

Maturity is understanding whether ego is the key to lose a relation and win an argument or it can be put to better use by doing vice-versa.

I crave intimacy, it's good.
It's very good.
Ah, our minds cummed at the
same time.

Sex is the best when both partners cum together in a flow and so is a relationship, when one was about to say something and other said it and both smiled at each other. Physical intimacy and its compatibility is good, but even if it's not, the relation can go forever. But if Mental intimacy & emotional intimacy is not good, the relation will come to an end whether without getting toxic or after getting toxic.

What excites me? Mind reading, Eye reading, Lip reading and over and above all, reading me when I'm trying my level best to hide it from you.

My switch on, your switch on: ON
My switch off, your switch on: OFF
My switch on, your switch off: OFF
My switch off, your switch off: ON

Science, maths, and the theory of love - all say if both sides are positive, it's positive. Even if both sides are negative, it's positive because in love, no one will get affected. But if one side is negative and the other is positive, the one who is positive (in love) will always have their switch off, or you can say, mood off.

One-sided love is like history which no one will read, except the one who is writing it.

We all do multiple things in life for just one thing i.e. to fulfil our expectations. What about our expectations in love relationships? You expect just one thing: equal love from both sides, or more love from one side and equal efforts from the other end. The problem is, not equal love because that hole can be filled by efforts, but the whole of one-sided love cannot be filled by either of them.

Cherry on the cake is HOPE, which, if not fulfilled, leaves a person with it, HOPELESS.

If the thought of someone else heated you up, let your thoughts be like water, tranquil in calm weather and vapour in heat. Do remember vapour comes back as water again when it rains.

When you get in a fight with someone and it ends up in a breakup, the thoughts of that person and the incident burns you up but you forget about them when you find someone better.

The problem is not getting such thoughts, the problem is regretting it later when you realize how futile it was to waste your energy. And you need a calm mind if you need to move on and to keep your search on for someone better.

We fail in multiple relationships with one complaint in common, "The other person changed."
Change is life's best friend. Make it yours too, otherwise you will feel your own life is your enemy.

We are never satisfied in relationships because we want our partner to love us the same way they loved us in the first week of us confessing to each other.

Love is the same but the way to showcase it changes. Your love for your mom is the same throughout, but maybe as you grow you are able to give her less time because of work commitments. Can't the same thing happen in relationships? Some changes are for good.

*I'm concerned for you that's why I won't
give you what you need,*

*I don't want you to get things which
your brain thought of last night,*

*I want you to learn the
'Art of Make It Happen.'*

I'm a Mumma's boy not because I wear the clothes which she selects, but because she is the keeper of my secrets.

Gen-Z children are more afraid of their fathers because most fathers are self-made man and want to give the same traits to their child. But fun is also necessary in life, and trust me, nothing can be more fun when a notorious teenager shares it all with his or her mother and she protects and guides them if they cross the boundaries.

Don't get upset girl, you are 'silver', But you got the 'silver-plated'.

You fall in love with someone on the first go but when you interact more, you realise that they don't possess the solid core values of life. This might make the relation unattractive to you before it starts. Sometimes you fall prey to people who are silver-plated, they don't have strong sentimental, emotional, spiritual values but they portray that they possess them. You misunderstand the plate to be gold and you ended up broken.

Do remember that silver is broken, melted, heated, or changed in shape but it's value never changes and in the end, in any shape, form etc it gets the same value and gold plating only helps it to gain higher value.

I want my dad to be my banker not my bank, I want him to say, "I bank you."

Gen-Z is a generation where there are professions more than doctors, engineers, lawyers, and CA. The amazing fact is that the new fields pay you more, maybe less money but more fun and happiness. We are a generation who wants to try new things and focus on exploring life more than settling in life.

Our father cares for us because no one knows the value of money better than them and they want us to get settled. Exploring may give results and help you make money if you excel in the field you choose. Trust me, the job becomes less difficult and you get immense support if your dad says, "I support you in whatever you do with all your heart and mind."

I lived with you and you taught me to live alone.

We all enjoy relationships because you become one from two. You live miles away, but both of you know about all your activities and daily course. When problems come in a relationship you try to solve them and sometimes overlook them, that's where the problem starts because you can compromise anything to live with them. You feel complete with them.

Take it as a life lesson, when you enjoy your own company to the fullest and know how to be happy alone, that is the time you will understand the extent to which someone else can take a position in your life. The choice is yours because you can either teach this to yourself or learn it from someone else. Living alone is a lifestyle.

Friend has the word <u>rien</u> in it, it means do it well or not at all!

You may like hanging out with someone, you like to party together or anything where you people are partners of the good time is not real friendship. I'm friends with you when I can talk my heart out loud to you.

You need friends and you need to be one, who not just chill together, but also face the heat together.

Want to be a man?
Tell your dad what you feel,
Go tell him "I love you!"
Why did your heart just say
"No, I cannot?"

You are sometimes very expressive or emotional, but saying "I love you" to your dad is beyond the power which emotions can ever give you. Not only for boys but also for girls, you are dad's princess still feel so afraid to say so? Why ? THERE IS NO REASON.

In every Indian family or anywhere around the world, dad is a pillar of strength. We should take a piece of that strength and give happiness to the person who has sacrificed his happiness for ours. The chances of him saying I love you too are much more than in your modern relationships, trust me.

If you fall for somebody in a day, it will either end too fast or go too far.

Sometimes someone hits you so hard that they force you to think about them. You might get attracted to someone's body or physical personality that you may never want them to go. You want to stay close to them but life has some other plans for you. Such relations last early if they are held with the attraction of the two bodies and not the two minds.

A relationship goes too far if in the first conversation, you have pleased your ears more than your eyes i.e. you are attracted to that person's thought process. These relations last forever or even beyond forever if they have inspired many from their compatibility.

Toxic relationships end with a few learnings, one learns how to make the next one more toxic but the other learns how to never get into a relationship and how to compare the habits of the next person to the last one. They then leave them because they don't fear losing love, they fear toxicity.

I became a mentor of love relationships, couldn't work out mine but learned a lot so thought of teaching and monetising it.

You learn more from your mistakes than success. Loving someone is not a mistake but crossing boundaries in hope that the other will also do the same is one. We should try to find positivity in everything and the best way to overcome your mistakes is by teaching others, so that they don't make the same mistakes .

You invested money in your relationship in the form of gifts, trips, etc. If it didn't work out, recover it back from mentorship. Create a community of failed lovers, the support of one another can make you do fun together. It is much needed.

My ex thought I'm gone.
I was still there, lonely in the paradise of
love,
finding love or self-love.

Sometimes it's hard to believe that someone whom we loved so much broke up with us. We sometimes feel that even if they don't love us back, they should stay so that we can love them. But that is not sustainable, because the day they will move on, you will be left with no one but yourself to love.

Sometimes we say 'break up and move on' together as if that's a term, but we fail to understand that 'move on' not always mean loving someone else. It sometimes means loving yourself when your ex falls for someone else.

I never thought she would take our joke of 'Love Story 2020' so seriously that we couldn't live more than a year together.

Sometimes we are so much into texting our partner that we say a lot of things, some things are meant to go with the flow and not discussed. Whenever we try to time things, the pressure builds and makes us do what we never wanted to do, why? Because it makes us overthink in the wrong direction. Don't celebrate anniversaries, rather celebrate the seconds you live together, because life changes in a second, not a year.

Dating means for a year or so because relation means forever.

The word is relation and not relationship in the quote intentionally because they both mean the same, but we sometimes forget that. Let's compare, you share a relation with your parents, siblings, cousins, best friends. Do you take that lightly? No, then why do we take the relationship with our partner lightly.

It's fine to be casual if you don't want to commit yourself forever. then don't call that relation a relationship, call it dating. If you are wondering under which category do boyfriends and girlfriends come, they come under the category of dating, because trust me, relationships don't need validation of the worldly words.

I have broken my hand,
I have broken my leg,
I have broken my heart,
The third one pains the fastest and the
longest.

Teenagers are taught to be extra cautious when they play sports, like 'play safely otherwise you will get hurt' but why aren't they taught about relationships? If they are taught how to not give themselves in a relationship, probably, they will save themselves from being heartbroken because here you don't play, you get played!

Trust me, I Love You!
Trust me you make it weaker when you say, trust me.

The self-doubt zone is not only for an individual, but also for a relationship, and when something like this happens, the last thing you should doubt is your love for each other. Sometimes, a relationship ends even when there is love on both ends, but compatibility is the culprit or something else. Every subject has a chapter where you feel stuck. In that case, you focus to improve in that chapter instead of doubting your understanding of the subject or your interest in it. Take compatibility or any other factor as the chapter and relationship as the subject. And trust me or not, everything will fall in place.

Giving fucks is the biggest fuck up in this fucking world!

When you care for someone, give attention, and show desperation to be with that person, your chance of losing value is higher than your chance of losing them. But is it worth staying in a place where you don't hold value? NO, so more than love try to find value for yourself. History is evidence to the fact that things which come easy aren't valued or considered the greatest possession of all times.

Fighting with someone doesn't mean you don't love that person. Take an example: Your sibling.

We learn the meaning of the word 'fighting' from the fights we have with our siblings during childhood, but as we grow older, we forget the real essence of it. We used to fight for the first hour and play together the second. Then why do we keep fights as a constant hurdle in our life in other relations which we make ourselves? Because we don't consider them family. You realize the value of a relationship when you value it over your stupid fights with them as in the case of family. Then only you are eligible to say, "You are family".

Bond. It's a contract which is done on a piece of paper. Don't say we have a bond, let it be felt by both the ends.

Bond is a contract with fixed interest rates but that's not what happens in a relationship. Relations cannot be bound by conditions; they can only be bound by the feelings of trust, care and love.

'It's not the bond you should be fond of, it's the feeling that you should have a craving for'.

My brain gives assistance to my whole body, even my heart, because it sometimes tends to take decisions blindly.

Every life decision, professional decision or personal decision must be thought of from the non-emotional zone before taking the final call. Our heart is not capable enough to think without emotions, and therefore, all decisions should flow through the King, the Mind.

Our heart flows the blood and it sometimes flows itself as a love bird, the mind or the brain are stronger than one can explain.

Sayings

Make your relationship the product of your thoughts, not

that of the opinion of others.

The story of every girl:

"You gift me flowers, chocolates, dresses, jewellery but you

know what makes me the happiest?

My Freedom!"

85

Either live in it or don't but never live with it.

Relationship with our family and friends is like a Fudge:

All sweet with a few nuts, sweetness adds the flavour, but

nuts add the beauty.

Whenever I ask my mom 'What do you want from me, I'm

going to this city,' she says:

"Drive slow, get back safely!"

People will say 'You are my biggest possession,' which you

are, but only for your Mom & Dad.

Drive slow, your one wrong overtake might make all the

difference to them.

I know you are counting the number of days

you haven't talked to them and

feeling, you will move on.

You will, the day you

will stop counting.

I value you more than I value my ego

that's why I say Sorry, not because I'm weak

Ours

Our > We are

'We are happy' is a statement where you have to inform others about your happiness and the people who are happy have a sense of individual happiness.

Our happiness is a more heart-felt statement where we derive happiness from each other. The people who are happy are happy with a sense of oneness and have a sense of synergy with each other.

Our world needs an (h)our of our day.

Now you think of our world, as your family and extended family, your country or earth, will decide how big and bright your thought process is. The irony is all three of them need an (h)our of our day.

Those who do amazing things in life are not those who didn't see bad phases, they have actually seen the worst, but they focus on the next positive not the last negative.

Dedication to lead,
Commitment to feed.

This is a life story of every leader, but the only difference is that they are taking complete responsibility of the risk but only a pie of the reward. Every time a leader does great they feel a sense of accomplishment, because while running an organization they are less worried about the profits, but more worried about the salary they will have to pay before the 7th of each month.

They learn not only to lead the company but also their brain, because they can't afford to let the situation control their brain. Brain is a tool which they keep a control over which in turn makes them the supreme leader of everything else.

Overthinking is right when you know what is wrong in overthinking.

You cannot revolutionise the world, the product, the process, the system, the human race until you overthink about what you are revolutionising. If you plan to revolutionise all the above stated things at once you will move in the wrong direction and reach the no man's land but if you stay dedicated and pick one, you will make the world, your country, your home a better place.

Overthink in the morning and oversleep in the same number of hours in the night or overthink in the night and you will not be able to outwork others in the morning. Sleep tight!

If we lose money,
we only lose money.
If we lose happiness,
We lose the chance to grow again.

You use money to get things which make you happy but imagine a day comes when you can buy anything which is sold, money won't make you happy. You think Elon Musk gets happiness by the money he makes? No, his happiness lies in the products he creates. Even if one day he loses all his money, he will use his happiness of creating new products to create those products which will in turn make him money.

Having more money or less money can have side effects but being happier will have none, if that happiness is not based on any parameter.

Horrified will soon be glorified.

Some people see a lot at a young age, maybe someone becomes an orphan, some lose their mom or dad or in other words, the person they loved the most in their life. These incidences leave us horrified but I'm sorry mate, look at the best artist or stars around you or on the silver screen their success story has the pain which made the glory worth more to them and helped them stay grounded.

Many of you won't be able to relate to this one but the one who can, STOP cursing yourself to lose them and look at the life story of whosoever is your favourite out of the three, Shah Rukh Khan, Cristiano Ronaldo or Virat Kohli.

Cheetah and the dogs

There was a race on the ground between 5 dogs and one cheetah. As the referee pressed the trigger of the gun, the cages opened and the dogs started running towards the finishing line to win the race but the cheetah didn't move an inch.

You know what happened next? The audience, the referee and the judges were only looking at the cheetah, which was sitting there as if the race was not for him.

Every action doesn't need a reaction. You might not gain respect by winning but by not playing, because the game was not for you but for those who look up to you but will never confess. I want to say one thing: Know your worth, show your work, and then grow your net-worth.

Life is next level beautiful! To see that, you need to be next level.

Satisfaction is the real game changer. We sometimes get too satisfied with what we have and don't focus on growth and the opposite of growth is decline. Many people think that if they don't grow they will be stagnant, but sooner or later we have to realise that the world is still growing, and if you don't, you wither.

The world is always more beautiful at the next level. For example, if you have seen Bali, eye to travel to Hawaii and if you have travelled the whole world, look at the vision of ELON MUSK, he is planning to create life on Mars. To end, I will say, day dreamers see all the levels at once, that is also wrong if you want to grow, just see the next level and then the next and then the next because 'the next' will never end.

The sun always shines, it's just that you can't see it sometimes.

The sun always shines. What matters is on which part of the Earth you are standing at. The same goes with life. Life will surely shine for you, depending on which part of it you are standing right now. For some, it shines early and for some, it shines late. It has one expectation from you i.e. to never Give up!

The people who work in the sun aren't afraid of heat and you have to take a lesson from that. You cannot be afraid of the heat you are facing at the moment, because it's a test which is won by those who don't burn.

The goal is to grow rich in life, in spirituality, in wisdom, in thoughts and in deeds.

Money? Let it stay in the pocket, because that is where it belongs.

Money is important, but many times it gets to. our brain and we forget, what one leaves behind for the world is not money, but legacy. We remember the world leaders like Abraham Lincoln, Mahatma Gandhi, and many others. Do we remember who was the then richest man on the planet? No, because richness comes by virtue of knowing how to lead life, not to live life.

Excuse or Refuse

We have a set priority list of people. To one we give an excuse, saying, "I have an exam next week and I cannot go out for dinner today" and to the other, we say, "I have an exam next week let's go out for dinner because I want to freshen my mood." The first situation is an example of an excuse, not refusal, but if we give it a deep thought it's actually refusal. Whenever you don't focus on your goal and try to give an excuse to yourself, just think that you are refusing to do that particular thing. Maybe it will give you a guilt trip and you will get back to work.

When you don't want something or someone, don't make an excuse, just refuse because excuse is a sign of the weak and refusal is a sign of the strong. The people who can say straight NO, have the power of decision making. It shows they don't run away from situations and arguments.

You showed it off,
I shared it all.

The worst thing one can do is to make someone look small in worth. This can only be done by those who think worth is decided by the money you made. There is always a way to do things and if you share your success story or success products like expensive cars, watches or houses with someone, humbleness should be there in your words and your actions.

Want to show off something? Show the world the strength of your relationships.

> ***Dogs are people's favourite pet animals because they show their affection by actions not by words. Humans should learn something from them, even that dog owner.***

The concept of texting has decreased the value of words, because in the flow, words stop meaning anything to the writer because texts don't show emotions at all. Therefore, the intensity of any relation looks the same from both ends over text, but the real difference comes when it's your turn to show actions or for that sake AFFECTION.

Delivery of everything in your life decides how the delivery of your life will be.

With the advent of e-commerce companies, delivery for us means product delivery, but in life anything you commit you have to deliver. Even if you say sorry to someone, you have to deliver i.e. not to make that mistake again. Everyone is a product of the accuracy of their delivery.

Here is a tip: If you want to deliver, know before committing how much you can deliver because over delivery is not a problem but overcommitment is.

In this technology world, you move from computer to laptop to iPad to iPhone. Just the goal is to be faster in processing and better in memory. Some people say technology is our life today and I said, "Technology is like our life". The goal is to be faster and sharper with each passing year.

History is not created by those who read history to create history and are not historians.

We live in a fast-moving world where everyday history is written and modified. Here, history doesn't only mean business or political history, but also the way people try the same old ways to become successful, which were used by others - maybe a way to get a higher package in salary or working on the same idea which was solved and scaled by someone else.

The people who create history and get famous among the masses are those who focus on innovation rather than just modification.

You want to achieve it by 32, to work for someone who is 28 and just thought of achieving it without putting an age bar to it.

We focus on achieving the goal according to a time span, or in a time span that brings on an added pressure. The power of pressure is like the power of compounding, but in a negative direction. When you have worked on something for 'X' days and '2X' days are left for the deadline, you will work well, but as you have spent '2X' days on something and 'X' days are left, you feel the pressure because you are nowhere near the goal. What if you leave all your hope to do it on completion of '3X' days and the goal was reachable in '3X+3' days?

You didn't lose to the goal, you lost to the timeline. And the pressure of the timeline makes you unproductive in the last few days, and therefore, you fail to achieve your goal.

I'm fond of reading,
The mind.

Every skill needs practice, but the skill of reading a person's mind needs the skill set of Presence of Mind. Using your presence of mind is a different ball game, because the important factors are not only to notice things about someone as it happens, but also to correlate it with the last one. For that, you need to store everything you noticed in your brain. The next step is to build synergy between all the points you stored in your brain from the past and the present and then predict the future, because if you can't predict the person's next move after reading their mind, there is no use in doing that in the first place.

Be the person who keeps changing between extrovert-ambivert-introvert depending on time-place-people-thing.

If we get a chance to select one, we should select to be an extrovert who speaks after thinking from their brain. But we should have a kind of changing speaking behaviour depending on the surroundings, because speaking and getting successful both requires the right use of your energy. The people who want to channelize in the right direction should prefer being an introvert in front of fools, who just want to show themselves as superior and disrespect others, because if you argue with them you will regret wasting energy later. Be an ambivert in front of knowledgeable people, because what you can learn from them by listening is more than what you can learn from speaking. And prefer being an extrovert in front of your peers, because that gives you an upper edge in the group you stand.

Present to the future- "I'm damn confused."
Future replied, "Same here, but I'm better than you."

We all stay confused in the current world because every day we have a new field to explore, new people to meet, new places to visit and new changes to make in ourselves and in the world around us. But in this confusion, we end up doing nothing but thinking about the future. Future is just the ultimate synergy between today, tomorrow and the day after, so, it means we will still be confused after three days but we will be better.

Either live today or live the future, I would say, live today and lead in the future.

The world is in need,
Do some good deeds.
Otherwise, we all will pay the fees,
In the form of our peace.

Even if we do good deeds, we expect some return out of it and I'm sure we will expect it from the world as well. We pay the rent for the property we stay in if we don't own it, but do we pay the final rent to Mother Earth for having taken up space on it and having made it so dirty? When you stay as a tenant and leave the flat you have to get it painted. When we leave the earth, we either create ashes, which again create pollution, or we become a part of earth and take a rent-free space on it forever. So when we are alive, we can at least do some good deeds and pay back what cannot be paid in money. Otherwise, be ready to get played with your peace because CORONA VIRUS was just the trailer of nature, the movie would be named "Clean Up Or Weep Up."

Talent is a Pond, Creativity is a Sea. Both of them together fabricates an Ocean whose 3D dimension is unlined.

If you find someone pretty good at something, they aren't God-gifted, it's the synergy between creativity and profession which is termed as talent. Sometimes, people stay good at something for a few years and then lose their charm, because they fail to understand that talent is unlined i.e. it has length, breadth and depth which cannot be measured not even by them in years.

Creativity means thinking out of the box. The day you will stop that, your thoughts will be compressed in a box, and if it happens with all worldly professions then the earth will become a box, not the explorer's own homeland.

Life gives me a challenge,
I said, "Let's go",
A fool gives me a challenge,
I said, "Let it go".

I'm fond of winning because I'm fond of working hard. That's why I take challenges seriously, provided those challenges make me better at some parameters which helps me grow in life. What can be better than being offered a challenge by life?

If you waste a second in proving yourself to the fool, you are a bigger fool. We sometimes fall prey to them and regret later, I don't want you to keep any regrets in life.

***Karma is a threat,
If you are double faced inside your chest.
Don't cause anyone pain,
If you want to make any gain.***

The worst thing one can do is, be someone else intentionally. You want something from someone? You want to please someone? Go straight up and ask for it or work for it. Wearing a mask and influencing people for your good and unmasking later will hurt them.

When Karma activates, it makes sure you deactivate because when you hurt someone, the dirt is on you and you have to clean it.

I use the brain, you use the Money.
You got the brain, I got the money.
We are even, just that I'm Self-Made.

Why do people remember the self-made more? Because they use the brain to make the money and then the money to build the wealth, the goal was never to get rich. They only gain in this process, even if their business fails, they get rich in experience. People who got the money, first make losses, and then get some brain which they use to cover up their losses and then make some money.

One thing which makes the person with brain valuable is their understanding of the value of money, because their whole money theory, till the time their money starts making money, is 'every penny earned is every penny saved' and INVESTED!

Sayings

We will understand the importance of savings

as we will grow old,

The way we realise it when our

phone is about to die.

*People laugh on memes and
videos made on girls being a gold digger.
Well I'm sorry, in the last six months,
I have come across many girls who are
'GOAL Diggers' not Gold Diggers!*

We should keep a control on our

Emotions and save our Energy at the

right place for the right time,

Emotions are 'Energy in motion'

so by keeping a check on our

emotions we will indirectly keep a

check on our energy outflow.

Man will be Men from being

Mumma's Boy to the Family Man.

The major problem with the GEN-Z is

that they always feel time is running out

and they are growing very fast.

It actually happens 'because you are being productive each

day and the day is over with one click.

It's good actually,

make your everyday count!

There are three types of people in the world:

1. The people who watch things happen.

2. The people who wonders what happen.

3. The people who make things happen.

The key to grow is to 'keep going'

no matter what stops you because

the tree near running water gives more fruits.

Defeat the situation, which is Tough,

by being Tougher so that you are

ready to face the Toughest!

To those who body shame themselves,

whenever you stand in front of the mirror,

talk to yourself before looking at your body

because that mind is your hidden treasure.

A treasure which is priceless.

We live life,

we weep life,

we greet life,

but in the end,

we need life.

Smile not always shows that we are happy,

It acts as a proof that times are tough

but we have faith in ourselves.

Many blame, Few claim.

Don't waste your time blaming,

Invest your time claiming.

Acknowledgements

"Success of one is success of many".

-Prafful Garg

A leader alone cannot complete the goal unless the team says yes, with all their heart and brain. My life in the last five years has been the same. I built two companies with a team of the same few people. And I have written this book with the support of the same people. But I will start with people because of whom I'm able to do all this. Thank you, mom, Mrs. EKTA GARG for always believing in me. I have talked about Mumma's boy in the book and I can't relate more. Thank you to my younger sister, Ms. SHUBHI GARG for being a constant support. Her placement in TCS during tough conditions of Covid-19 has been an inspiration for me.

I would like to thank Mr. SHIVAS BEHL, COO of Younity.in, for being my constant support in this journey of book writing. Thank you Mr. SUNNY TAKRANI, CMO at letsbookmypg.com, for being my constant support in whatever new I do. Thank you team ANUJ JAIN, JAANAVI BAKSHI and everyone else from my YOUNITY.in and LETSBOOKMYPG.com family.

My friends have been my biggest critics. I would like to thank AMBUJ SHARMA, OJASVA CHUGH, SUYASH GUPTA and SIDDHARTH KALRA for being my support system.

Special thanks to PRANJAL SACHDEVA, who had more trust in me than I had in myself and for bringing me this idea of writing a book after seeing my journey of building a 21,000 strong Instagram family with my content on @praffulgarg. I would also like to thank the photographer, SANJAY SHARMA sir. He is one of the best photographers of Delhi and his creation on the cover just proved that right. He is highly skilled and a thorough professional.

Last but not the least I would like to thank my community, Younity.in's community members YouKnights for always trusting me, respecting me, and motivating me to do new things in life. The 9 PM sessions I take have been my biggest motivator to write this book.

The next book will be out on July 9th 2021, the day I will be celebrating my 24th birthday with a family much bigger than ever after the release of this book.

About the Author

Prafful Garg is a young entrepreneur who did his graduation in Business Economics from University of Delhi. He is the founder & CEO of letsbookmypg.com, a student accommodation company which recently celebrated its 4th Foundation Day on 15th August 2020 and Younity.in, India's biggest Digital Student Community with the Foundation Day on 6th March 2020, the release day of this book. Younity.in has more than 11,000 community members pan-India where he takes online sessions on various Professional and Personal topics like Group Discussion, Public Speaking, Personal Interviews, Overthinking, Emotional Balance, Eve-Teasing, Sex Education, Heart vs Mind and much more. Keeping his vision on the holistic development of the students and bringing a change in the thought process of the youth of India.

Prafful has been dignified with the prestigious REX-Karmaveer GYLC Award 2019 (Institute by United Nations) at IIT-Delhi. In 2016, at the age of 21, he successfully raised Rs. 3.5 crore from an Angel Investor. He has also been invited in more than 200 public speaking events at various prestigious institutes like IIM Indore, IIM Rohtak, Hansraj College, Hindu College, and many more across the country.

Over the time he has gained immense love and support from his 21,000 strong Instagram family by his regular content on @praffulgarg. Prafful has also been featured and quoted in various leading E-papers and news magazines like Education Times, India Today and Your story.

INKFEATHERS PUBLISHING

India's Most Author Friendly Publishing House

Stay updated about latest books, anthologies, events, exclusive offers, contests, product giveaways and other things that we do to support authors.

 Inkfeathers Publishing

 @InkfeathersPublishing

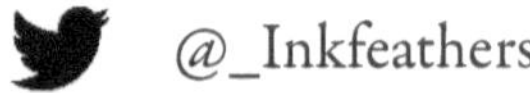 @_Inkfeathers

 @Inkfeathers

 Inkfeathers.com

We'd love to connect with you!